From the Lowest River Valley to the Highest Mountain Peak

By Rabbi Hector, Evelyn Gomez,
and David C. Malberg

WestBow Press books may be ordered through booksellers or by contacting:

WestBow Press
A Division of Thomas Nelson & Zondervan
1663 Liberty Drive
Bloomington, IN 47403
www.westbowpress.com
1 (866) 928-1240

ISBN: 978-1-4908-4823-5 (sc)
ISBN: 978-1-4908-4822-8 (e)

Library of Congress Control Number: 2014914942

Printed in the United States of America.

WestBow Press rev. date: 8/25/2014

WESTBOW
PRESS
A DIVISION OF THOMAS NELSON
& ZONDERVAN

Contents

ACKNOWLEDGMENTS

This book is dedicated to the 15ᵗʰ Anniversary of Relationship Enrichment Center, Beit Tikkun, in Tampa, Florida.

This is the ministry of Rabbi Hector, Pastor Evelyn, Sarah, Jeremy, and Eric Gomez.

The book is also a work of non- fiction. It chronicles critical events. Several names have been changed to protect their identity.

DavidMalberg

Thanks to my **Rabbi Hector Gomez** and his wife, **Pastor Evelyn Gomez**, and my wife, **Holly Malberg**, for their encouragement, prayer, and support for this literary project.

Pictures were provided by **Sarah Gomez**.

David

PREFACE

The focus of this book is to show the continuation of deliverance from a stronghold of anger in *David* (*Taavi*) and a stronghold of fear in Holly (*Susan*).

We began to walk in the principles of **Torah** in the beginning of June, 5773 (Hebrew calendar). We went back to tithing the gross and giving to the "Needs Fund (Benevolence)" at R.E.C., Beit Tikkun in Florida. *[www.recministries.org]*

In the Year 5774, 'Ayin Dalet', {6014} , [2014], *Rabbi* shared that this year, because of number four (4), letter 'Dalet', "there would be open doors for us to leap forward". There will be "notable miracles leaping forth".

Later, *Rabbi Gomez* (Ya'akov) encouraged *David* (Taavi) to learn the **shofar**. Sounding this instrument has brought about physical and spiritual healing and financial blessing to the *Malberg* (Mohler) household.

Also, during the first month of their attendance at R.E.C., the Malbergs (*Mohlers*) became involved with the prayer group on Tuesday night. The precious group of believers include: *Pastor Evelyn* (Debra) *and Linda* . Later, at times, *Irma, Flavio, Alex and Sarah* would join us. Also, *Ceci, Carlos, Betty, and Lisa* attended some prayer sessions.

Also, during the operations and trials of our faith, the Rabbi's children: *Sarah* and *Jeremy* (Jeremiah) prayed for us, along with *Kenny and Kim, Diane, Edna, Janice, Chuck and Charles.* <u>Frank</u> and <u>Hylon</u> encouraged *David* (Taavi) with the shofar.

Thanks to *Rosario Sena* and his shofar classes. *Carla Adams* also had financial classes, for which we give thanks.

We enjoyed suppers after **Shabbat** with *Marilyn*, from Georgia, and others at *Village Inn*.

The **Lord** had blessed the *Malbergs* (Mohlers) in their former church of forty years, where they were active in many roles; but, **Adonai** led the family to the ministry of *Rabbi Gomez* and his family through their daughter *"Rachel."*

This story is a continuation of the testimony of deliverance for *Taavi* in "**Joy from the Ashes**" and the family search for their **Hebrew roots** in "**Sanctuary Lake Home**".

Scripture and sources related to *Rabbi Hector Gomez* and his research, and original music lyrics will be used to illustrate each part of the testimony.

Also, there are other sources quoted.

The "*New Living Translation*" version of the **Holy Bible** will be used with selected chapters and verses.

The "*New Jerusalem Bible*" version of the **Holy Bible** will also be used with selected chapters and verses.

INTRODUCTION

"I want to thank David and Holly Malberg for having the courage and sensitivity to embrace their *Hebrew Roots* for such a time as this! In their quest to grow spiritually, they have embraced **God's Holy Word,** the **Torah**, and the **Sabbath!**

It brings me great joy, that in all their years of serving **God,** they have finally realized the truth about the **Sabbath!** They have embraced the revelation of **God's Sabbath** from Friday Sundown to <u>Saturday Sundown.</u>

David and Holly have shared with me, many times, how much they have learned in **God's Word** since they have joined the *Relationship Enrichment Center, Beit Tikkun – House of Restoration* in Tampa, Florida.

David's [second] book was also birthed while attending our congregation. [His first book was *Sanctuary Lake Home* and was birthed at <u>R.E.C.</u>] It is well written so that it will bring every reader a great sense of joy and appreciation for the **Torah** and the **Feast Days** and **Betrothal."**

<u>A personal note to David and Holly</u>: "Thank you again for opening your heart to **Yeshua Messiah,** and I know that you will be a great influence not only to your family, but to everyone you reach with with your book!

Your joy and love for **God**, by embracing the *Hebrew Roots* of the *Christian Faith* will leave a legacy for all the future generations.

We pray **God's Blessings** for you and your family; and, Evelyn and I look forward to having a greater relationship with you and your family in the years to come!"

In Yeshua Messiah's Service,

Rabbi/Pastor Hector & Evelyn Gomez

Chapter 1

OUT OF EGYPT

On June 8, the *Mohlers, Taavi and Susan*, began attending **R.E.C., Beit Tikkun**. It was Rabbi *Ya'akov's* (Hector's) birthday. He spent time at our table, for which we thought was remarkable at the time.

He also gave us some prayers for casting down of strongholds. These prayers are declarations of the power of **the whole armor of God**. They also involve binding the Accuser and his kingdom and breaking generational curses. We ask that we be delivered from evil and that **Yeshua c**over us with His blood. We submit ourselves and our families to the ministry of the **Holy Spirit.**

James 5: 13 -16: 13"Are you suffering hardships? You should pray. Are any of you unhappy? You should sing praises. 14Are any sick? You should call for the elders of the church to come and pray over you, anointing you with oil in the name of the **Lord**. 15Such a prayer offered in faith will heal the sick, and the **Lord** will make you well. And if you have committed any sins, you will be forgiven. 16Confess your sins to each other and pray for each other so that you may be healed. The earnest prayer of a righteous person has great power and produces wonderful results." *[NLT]*

Leaving a traditional church, which celebrated the **Sabbath** on Sunday, and celebrating the **Lord's Sabbath** from **Friday at sundown to Saturday at sundown** was an interesting transition for the *Mohlers*. However, in **Genesis 2, verses 2 – 3** , the **Bible** states: 2"On the seventh day **God** had finished **his work of creation**, so he rested [ceased] from **all his work**. 3And **God blessed the seventh day and declared it holy**, because it was the day when he rested from all **his work of creation**." *[NLT]*

Also, **Exodus 35: 2***:* "You have six days each week for your ordinary work, but the seventh day must be a **Sabbath** day of complete rest, **a holy day** dedicated to the **Lord**." *[NLT]*

Also, the *Mohlers* began, within the month of June, to attend the Tuesday night prayer meeting.

The family began giving of their gross income, according to **Malachi 3:10** : 10"Bring all the tithes into the storehouse so there will be enough food in my **Temple**. If you do, 'says the **Lord of Heaven's Armies**. 'I will open the windows of heaven for you. I will pour out a blessing so great you won't have enough room to take it in! Try it! Put me to the test!" *[NLT]*

Also, the *Mohlers* started giving regularly to the "*Needs Fund*" for the church. This fund is managed by *Pastor Evelyn* (Debra).

The Torah also has certain dietary laws that *Taavi* and *Susan* began to follow. The **Bible**, in the **Tanakh**, states what animals that can be used for food (see **Leviticus 11**). In **Leviticus 11: 46-47** the **Bible** states: 46"These are the instructions regarding land animals, birds, marine creatures, and animals that scurry along the ground. 47By these instructions you will know what is unclean and clean, and which animals may be eaten and which may not be eaten." *[NLT]*

Another addition to the devotions of the family are the "*Amidah*" prayers, given at 9 A.M., noon, and 3 P.M. According to information compiled by *Rabbi Gomez* (Ya'akov): " the word '*Amidah*' literally means 'standing' because it is recited while standing. The praying three times a day was established by *Ezra* and codified in the *Talmud*, Berakhot 26b. The prayers are powerful and they become everyone's personal prayer: wealth and health are two needs. The custom is to face the direction of **Israel** (East). This shows respect for the **Temple** and reminds one that the synagogue was established to attempt to fill the gap in **Hebrew** life left by the **Temple's** destruction."

Toward the end of the month of June, the **Lord** gave *Taavi* the inspiration for the completion of "*Sanctuary Lake Home*", for which *Rabbi Hector* (Ya'akov) wrote a foreword, along with *Pastor Evelyn* (Debra), his wife.

The *Mohlers* began, also, to attend "**Torah Studies**" on Thursday evening.

At the same time, Taavi wrote his first **Messianic** song: "**Praise Adonai o my Soul**" *(Psalm 146 & II Samuel 6:12-15).*

Intro: "**Halleluyah! Praise Adonai** o my soul! I will praise **Yeshua** forever. **Blessed is Messiah**!

Verse 1: I will sing songs to my **God** for all my life! Happy is he who gets help from the **God of Ya'akov.**

Verse 2: David danced before the **Lord** with trumpet blasts! **Israel** shouted as they brought the **Ark of Adonai!**

Chorus: **Yahweh** is in charge forever! **He is Tziyon's God! He** is for all generations. **Praise be to Yehovah!**" *[©2013 Malberg]*

The **Lord** gave *Taavi* another song:"**My Savior Who is my Shepherd**" *(Psalm 23)*:

"**My Savior** who is my **Shepherd** allows me to be content always! From quiet pools, I drink. **He** guides me to right paths for **His Name's sake**! . **Amen. Praise Him! His guiding hand** always protects. **He** is with me. Dinner is served. My cup is blest. **Mercy** is set. **Life** is with **Yahweh** forev'r." *[©2013 Malberg]*

Chapter 2

IN THE WILDERNESS

Another new thing for *Taavi* and *Susan* is the **Sabbath Feast**, celebrated at **sundown on Friday night.** This celebration has proven to be a great blessing for the Mohlers. They pray the "**Shema**" prayer each Friday evening. Also, in the services at R.E.C., Beit Tikkun, Rabbi Gomez leads us in this prayer:

"Sh'ma Yisrael, Adonai, Elohenu, Adonai Echad, Baruch Shem, K'vod malchuto, l'olam vaed."

"Hear o Israel, the Lord our God. The Lord is One, Blessed be His Name. His Kingdom is forever, and foreve rmore." (Mark 12:29)

"*Sh'ma Yisrael*" is sometimes called a rallying cry by Messianic Christians and it is a center piece of their Worship Service. It is a profession of faith and an affirmation of the unity of God.

This is a time of family fellowship, feasting, blessing, and edification which brings us closer to **Yahweh**, our **Adonai.**

The month of July began with an accident on a country road near their home. *Susan* was driving to work when a large commercial van backed up (about 10 – 15 MPH) and hit the *Mohler's* vehicle. *Susan* called *Taavi*, who came immediately.

The whole front section of the vehicle was destroyed. *Susan* complained of neck pain.

She decided to go to work and then to an urgent care orthopedic center. [They would not know the extent of *Susan's* injury until the second week of August.]

A **scripture** for this occasion: *John 17:33* : **Yeshua (Jesus)** said "**I** have told you all this so that you may have peace in me. Here on earth you will have many trials and sorrows. But take heart, because **I** have overcome the world." *[NLT]*

Taavi called the insurance company and arranged for the vehicle to be towed to a repair center. He also obtained a rental vehicle. They also sought out legal advice and recourse.

Later on, at the end of the month, the *Mohlers* went on vacation. The second day, *Susan* was feeling faint, somehow made it to the bathroom, and hit her head on the sink, and passed out, after she got to the bedroom.

Needless to say, *Taavi* called the emergency line and an ambulance was dispatched immediately. She was taken to the closest hospital, but because of the extent of her injuries with her jaw broken in three places, she was transferred to a hospital in a downtown location.

The first day and night, she was scheduled for surgery; but, other patients came in with extreme emergencies, and her surgery was postponed. However, *Dr. Kenyon* sewed up her tongue, which had been cut in her fall at the hotel.

She finally had her surgery: "***closed induction and maxillomandibular fixation***." This procedure involved placing wires in *Susan's* mouth to secure her jaw.

While she was in the hospital, *Rachel*, their daughter took turns in watching *Susan*. *Taavi* would cover the day time and *Rachel* covered the night hours, sleeping in the room with her mother, *Susan*. Taavi had to put their sweet creature kids, *Missy* (cockapoo dog) and *Jordie* (long-haired American cat) into the kennel.

The first day, after the operation, *Pastor Evelyn* (Debra) and *Linda* from *R.E.C.* came to see *Susan*. They brought a beautiful bouquet of flowers. *Susan, Taavi and Rachel* were blessed by this expression of love!!!

Sometime, later that evening, *Susan* fell in the bathroom at the hospital. *Rachel* called the nursing staff. *Susan* was transferred to *ICU*, where, over the course of many days, she had three transfusions. (It was discovered that *Susan* had anemia when she fell at the cottage.)

The *Mohlers* really appreciated all the prayers at *R.E.C., Beit Tikkun*.

Susan was released about a week after she was admitted to the hospital in a city across the Bay.

Another scripture: **Romans 5:3-5**: 3"We can rejoice, too, when we run into problems and trials, for we know that they help us develop endurance. 4And endurance develops strength of character, and character strengthens our confident hope of salvation. 5And this hope will not lead to disappointment. For we know how dearly **God** loves us, because **he** has given us the **Holy Spirit** to fill our hearts with **his love**." *[NLT]*

Chapter 3

CROSSING OVER

The second week of August, when *Susan* and *Taavi* returned from *Susan's* hospitalization across the Bay, there was an appointment with the *Orthopedic Doctor Antonio* and his assistant *Chuck*. It was determined that *Susan* had to wear a brace at all times until her surgery. She had to wear it in the house as well., and during sleeping.

Needless to say, *Susan* had to take a short-term leave of absence from her work. The insurance company approved the funds for her use during the time of her leave.

She also applied for lost wages from her employer. The result of that request will be shared in another chapter.

There were other financial blessings: 1) Received $500.00 for deduction from auto insurance. And 2) Received $1000.00 from AAA for hospitalization.

In the meantime, there were trips to the *Oral Surgeon Kenyon* at the *Bay City* every week for tightening and adjusting her wires and bands. *Taavi* made smoothies and purees for *Susan* each day, as she could only drink from a straw during this time.

The scripture for this physical challenge is found in ***Romans 8:28***: "And we know that **God** causes everything to work together for the good of those who love **God** and are called according to **his purpose** in them." *[NLT]*

I Peter 2:24 - 25 states: 24"**He** personally carried our sins in **his body** on the cross so that we can be dead to sin and live for what is right. **By his wounds you are healed**. 25Once you were like sheep who wandered away. But now you have turned to **your Shepherd, the Guardian of your souls.**" *[NLT]*

Taavi and *Susan* crossed over and are becoming **Hebrews** in the **Messianic Christian** movement.

Rabbi Gomez (Ya'akov) has some insight into this movement: " '**The Hebrew Roots of our faith'** are about learning the true language of the **Spirit of God**, and knowing **His thoughts, His mind**. Also, it is about truly knowing who is **Yeshua, Jesus our Messiah and Lord**!" "The **Bible** was written in **Hebrew** by **Hebrews**. **Hebrew** means '*crossover*' from '*Pagan Idolatry Worship*.'"

Yeshua was a first century **Jew.**

Excerpts from *Rabbi Hector* (Ya'akov): "**Messianic Judaism's** highest authority must be the **Bible/ Torah** (**'God's Teaching and Instruction'**) & that it must be objectively understood in the context of the original language in which it was revealed".

According to various scholars, every portion of the **Old** and **New Testaments** were written in **Hebrew** and **Aramaic.** We need to understand the **Bible** from this perspective.

An interesting fact is that *Taavi* bought a "***Complete Jewish Bible***" several years before he and *Susan* began attending *R.E.C.*

Concepts learned from *Rabbi Gomez:* "We are the **temple of Yahweh**, **the living God**, and **He** wants to live inside of us."

Also: "Walking in the **Torah**" is a way of life. This is the **Lord's plan** for us after we received **Salvation.**

In **R.E.C., a Messianic Christian church**, we follow the "**Biblical Feast Days**". These include: **Pesach (Passover), Shavuot (Pentecost), Yom Kippur (The Day of Atonement), Sukkot (Feast of Tabernacles), the time of the Lord's birth , and the weekly Sabbath from sun-down Friday to sun-down Saturday.**

From a source, '*Empowered by Christ*': "The **Hebrew Roots movement** (*H.R.M.*) is a contemporary global spiritual movement and advocates the return and adherence to the first century faith of **Jesus Christ [Yeshua HaMaschiach]** by seeking a better understanding of the culture.

The Ebionites (heretics) of the early church were part of '*HRM*'. They looked to **Yeshua** as **Messiah**, but also followed Jewish religious laws and rites.

Today '*HRM*' believes in the **Torah** as a foundation . Their basis is that **Yeshua** came to fulfill the **Torah** as **YHVH**'s plan of completion."

We believe in **Yeshua as Savior**. We also follow the dietary laws in *Leviticus* and keep the **Sabbath** holy (fourth commandment). We celebrate **Jewish feast days** and enjoy a **Messianic** style of worship with **Davidic** dances and blowing of the *shofar.*

We finish this chapter with *Psalm 111: 10*: "The **fear of the Lord** is the foundation of true wisdom. All who obey **his commandments** will grow in wisdom. **Praise him forever!**" *[NLT]*

Chapter 4

ROSH HASHANAH AND YOM KIPPUR

The *Mohlers* continued to travel back and forth across the Bay each week to have *Susan's* wires and bands adjusted. However, *Taavi* and *Susan* attended as may services as they could at *Beit Tikkun*.

"*The Feast Day* of **Rosh Hoshanah,** also known as the **Feast of Trumpets,** for 5774 signifies a time to come of **The Resurrection of the Dead and the Rapture of Believers**. It also relates to the **coronation of the Messiah** and the **wedding of the Messiah**. It is the beginning of a period of *soul-searching*, known as the **High Holy Days**, ending on **Yom Kippur**.

Prayers of thanksgiving are offered to **God** for **His great supply** during the year. Our faith is the center of attention. We focus on our relationship with **God**, asking forgiveness for our transgressions.

Also, there is the blowing of **the Shofar** for this celebration of the **Jewish New Year**." ("*The Jewish Holidays" by* **Strassfeld**)

Rabbi Hector: "**Yom Kippur** is, traditionally, when **the books of life and death are sealed**, and *Jewish people* will receive their coming judgment. The *traditional greeting* for this holiday is '**G'mar chatima tovah**!' or 'May you be sealed in the **Book of Life** for a good year!'

"**Yom Kippur** is also known as the **Day of Atonement**. '*Yom*' means '*day*' and '*Kippur*' means '*covering*' and '*atonement*'."

Leviticus 23:26-28: 26 'Then the **Lord** said to Moses': 27 "Be careful to celebrate the **Day of Atonement** on the tenth day of the same month –nine days after the **Festival of Trumpets**. You must observe it as an official day for holy assembly, a day to deny yourselves [or to fast] and present special gifts to the **Lord**. 28 Do not work during the entire day because it is the **Day of Atonement**, when offerings of purification are made for you, making you right with the **Lord Your God**." *[NLT]*

Rabbi Gomez : "Rabbis interpret '*deny yourselves*' to mean that we must restrain from our earthly appetites." "Another commandment is that *we are to do no work*. This day is called the '**Sabbath of Sabbaths**'. We are not to mix our daily routine with this holy day. The punishment for not obeying this commandment is death...*spiritually dead with no spiritual fruits*."

"The next commandment that **God** gave us is that we are to present **Him** an offering...we honor our **High Priest Yeshua** by our **Yom Kippur offerings**, which were to be *the very best that we* can *give!* **The Biblical Law** states that we are to give this special offering to **Adonai our Lord** on **Yom Kippur** because **Yeshua** was the very best **Offering** given to us for our **Atonements of sins!**"

It was not easy for *Taavi* and *Susan* to fast for twenty-four hours. *Susan* couldn't because she was still only drinking smoothies and eating purees. *Taavi* had a piece of fruit during the day.

One blessing came when the *best Offering* was presented. The **Lord** showed *Taavi* and *Susan* to give 10% of the amount from *a certain savings account*. This resulted in a 500% to 1000% *increase* for them. These details will be shared in upcoming chapters.

Chapter 5

SUKKOT

During this time, from the end of September to the beginning of October, this festival of **Sukkot** teaches the joy of the **Messianic Kingdom**: a daily rest (**Shabbat**) in the **Messiah** and rest *(menuchah)* of **His Kingdom** in our hearts.

In *Leviticus 23: 33 – 36*: 33'And the **Lord** said to Moses', 34 "Give the following instructions to the people of **Israel**. Begin celebrating the **Festival of Shelters** [or *Booths* or *Tabernacles*] on the fifteenth day of the appointed month—five days after the **Day of Atonement**. This festival to the **Lord** will last for seven days. 35On the first day of the festival you must proclaim an official day for **holy assembly**, when you do no ordinary work. 36 For seven days you must present special gifts to the **Lord.** The eighth day is another **holy day** on which you present your special gifts to the **Lord.** This will be a solemn occasion, and no ordinary work may be done that day."*[NLT]*

The people of **Israel** lived in booths when they were in the wilderness after they left Egypt. They entered the **Promised Land** with great rejoicing!!!

It is estimated that our **Savior, Yeshua HaMaschiach,** was born during the **Feast of Tabernacles (Sukkot)** on *September 29, BCE 2*. This thrilled *Taavi* because this day and month is also his birthday!

Because there was no room in the Inn, **Yeshua's** parents found a **Sukkah**, or booth, for the **Christ** child to be born: Luke 2: 4-7: 4"And because *Joseph* was a descendant of **King David**, he had to go to **Bethlehem** in **Judea**, **David's** ancient home. He traveled there from the village of **Nazareth** in **Galilee**. 5He took with him, *Mary,* his fiancée, who was now obviously pregnant. 6And while they were there, *the time came for her baby to be born.* 7She gave birth to her **first child** and laid him in a manger, because there was no lodging available for them."*[NLT]*

Taavi and *Susan* have a large umbrella and table on their patio. They put sheets of different colors to make their **Sukkah**. They ate several evening meals there, including a *Sabbath feast. Rabbi Hector* approved.

Also, at **R.E.C., Beit Tikkun,** a **Sukkah** was placed on the sanctuary property. There was a joyful gathering of parishioners, including the *Mohler's* son *David* with his family and daughter *Rachel.*

During this time, the *Mohler's* pool heater needed replacement. They were able to save $1500. on a new unit, with a ten year warranty.

Also, *Susan* was able to get comparable coverage of auto insurance (for renewal) with a savings of $1,000. How great is our God!!!

Also, during this time, *Taavi's* book, birthed and inspired by the ministry of the Holy Spirit at R.E.C., "**<u>Sanctuary Lake Home</u>**" was published October 1.

Rabbi Hector Gomez and *Pastor Evelyn* graciously agreed to write a *foreword* for his *[Taavi's]* book, which blessed him and encouraged him greatly!

Every week prior to *Susan's* cervical (neck) surgeries, *Taavi* had taken *Susan* to *Dr. Kenyon* across the Bay to have wires and bands adjusted, and finally removed.

The end of October (21 and 23), two critical and extremely life supporting neck surgeries were performed by *Dr. Antonio* and his medical team.

For the first operation, on October 21, there was a surgery described as : a ***"disketomy, anterior, with decompression of spinal cord and/or nerve roots."*** It also included: ***"Osteophytectomy; cervical, interspace arthrodesis, anterior interbody technique."***

The second operation was performed , on October 23: an ***"arthrodesis, posterior or posterolateral technique, single level; cervical below C2 segment; laminectomy, facetectomy, and foraminotomy"***. There is additional scientific information related to this procedure.

Rabbi Hector visited *Susan* during these surgeries and met *David*, the *Mohler's* son.

One scripture on which *Rabbi* encouraged us to take a stand is in ***Isaiah 53:4-5***: 4"Yet it was **our weaknesses he carried**; it was **our sorrows that weighed him down**. And **we thought his troubles were a punishment from God, a punishment for his own sins!** 5 But he was pierced **for our rebellion, crushed for our sins. He was beaten so we could be whole. He was whipped so we could be healed."** *[NLT]*

The Saturday before *Susan* was to be released, she developed complications.

Taavi went to the first part of **Shabbat** and had prayer. *Rabbi* also prayed with him.

Why would he leave his wife at the hospital at her time of suffering?

However because of his act of faith and petition to **Yeshua,** the next day, *Susan* was released . She had been in the hospital one week.

Adonai answered prayer!!! *Alleluyah*!!!

Chapter 6

THANKSGIVING

Susan was taken home. However, within the next several days, some respiratory problems were revealed; and after several different visits to two hospitals the same day, the second one at Fletcher admitted her. This would have been on Tuesday, the 29th of October.

It was discovered she contracted pneumonia in the hospital, while she was recovering from neck surgery.

Taavi and *Rachel* and *David* rotated visitation hours with *Susan* during this time.

Around *Susan's* birthday, *Taavi* was visiting *in Susan's* room. He developed chest pain. He was taken to the E.R. and admitted.

Taavi and *Susan* visited each other in their hospital outfits while *Taavi* was being evaluated. He had been under a lot of stress from the time of the accident the beginning of July through many surgeries, and now, pneumonia. Fortunately, he was released in time to attend **Shabbat** the second day of November.

Again, why would *Taavi* go to the altar and pray while his wife was still in the hospital? Again, **our Savior and Lord** intervened, and *Susan* was taken home the following Sunday.

He is faithful!!! Praise His Holy Name!!!

A few days later, *Susan* was severely constipated. She saw her regular *Doctor* for remedies. Within a day or so, it was obvious that traditional remedies were not working. So, again, *Taavi* took *Susan* back to *Fletcher hospital E.R.*

Dr. Meier did a "**manual disimpaction**" (after an xray revealed the source of her difficulty). *Susan* was given medicine and sent home to rest.

Because *Taavi* and *Susan* had made a commitment to obey the principles of the **Torah**, a life-time commitment, the Accuser had tried to take *Susan's* life.

This is why *Rabbi Hector Gomez* stronghold prayers were so important, as they were prayed daily and weekly. Also, attending *Tuesday evening prayers, Torah studies, and Shabbat* kept the *Mohlers* on track spiritually.

Taavi enjoyed the heated pool (92 degrees) the day of *Susan's* return home. Also, that evening, the temperature came down to 56 degrees. *Taavi* put a fire log into the fireplace. This was a tremendous blessing. [It was the first time that the fireplace had been used since March, earlier in the year.]

Other blessings occurred the day that Susan returned home: 1) A banana tree (given to the *Mohlers* by a neighbor) had produced two bunches of small bananas. 2) Tomato plants were overflowing with fruit and the Romaine lettuce had become ready to pick.

A financial blessing occurred also during this time, probably as a result of blowing the shofar and giving the first fruit offering on **Yom Kippur.** The *Mohlers* received $5700. for lost wages to *Susan* from their auto insurance company! *Isn't **Adonai** good to us!!!*

Within a day or two after *Susan* came back from the hospital the last time, *Pastor Evelyn* and *Linda* blessed the *Mohlers* with a fantastic meal! They need to know what a blessing that was to the *Mohlers* and how much of an encouragement!!! May they be blessed for their compassion and thoughtfulness!!!

Colossians 3:16-17: 16"Let the message about **Christ**, in all its richness, fill our lives. Teach and counsel each other with all the wisdom he gives. Sing psalms and hymns and spiritual songs to **God** with thankful hearts. 17And whatever you do or say, do it as a representative of the **Lord Jesus,** giving thanks through him to **God the father.**" *[NLT]*

Chapter 7

HANUKKAH

A wonderful thing occurred to *Taavi*. *Rabbi Hector* had suggested to him to purchase a shofar from Israel. *Taavi* began to blow that musical instrument in their home. This resulted in healing for *Susan*, peace and joy for the household, and financial blessing.

Taavi sounds the *shofar* three times a day at 9 A.M., noon, and 3 P.M. And he always, sometimes with *Susan* (when she is at home), recites the **Amidah** prayers at these times.

For a series of four weeks, from middle November to December, *Sr. Rosario* of the Spanish Ministry held *shofar* lessons. *Taavi* attended these meetings with great interest. This was a wonderful blessing.

Rosario explained the different sounds of the **shofar**: " 1)'*tek'iah*' –a long continuous burst. 2) '*shevarim*' ---it consists of three shorter blasts. 3) '*teruah*' –nine short bursts of a staccato blast. The first sound is of joy and happiness. The second and third sounds represent sadness, pain, and suffering. After the second and third sounds, we sound a *teki'iah* again to signify that **God i**s there, and in **His Mercy** will help us return to a state of jubilation again." {**torah.org**}

In the battle of Jericho, *Joshua 6: 4-5:* "₄ Seven priests will walk ahead of the **Ark**, each carrying a ram's horn. On the seventh day you are to march around the town seven times, with the priests blowing the horns. ₅When you hear the priests give one long blast on the rams' horns, have all the people shout as loud as they can. Then the walls of the town will collapse, and the people can charge straight into the town." *[NLT]*

Our **Adonai Elohim** will come back to earth sounding the **shofar**. *Zechariah 9:14:* "The **Lord** will appear above his people; his arrows will fly like lightning! **The Sovereign Lord** will sound the ram's horn and attack the whirlwind from the southern desert." *[NLT]*

According to *Leo Rosten* (*The Joys of Yiddish*), "The bend in the *shofar* is supposed to represent how a human heart, in true repentance, bends before the Lord. The ram's horn serves to remind the pious how *Abraham*, offering his son in Isaac in sacrifice, was reprieved when **God** decided that *Abraham* could sacrifice a ram instead. The man who blows the *shofar* is required to be of blameless character and conspicuous devotion; he must blow blasts of different timbre, some deep, some high, some quavering."

The middle of December, *Rosario* presented certificates in the **Shabbat** morning service with Hispanic pastor, *Pastora Monica*. There was a blessing for all of the students, including *Jorge*, *Pastora's* husband.

Susan was able to attend **Shabbat** for the first time since before her surgery on October 21, several weeks after she got home from her last hospital visit. [*Rabbi Ya'akov* had a vision of *Susan* earlier in the year, during her hospitalizations, that "she had her hands raised up high in praise and that she was energetically praising the Lord in the sanctuary"!!!]

***The Lord is great and greatly to be praised!!!* This vision came true in its entirety!!!**

Susan was able to drive home from the **Shabbat** a few days before ***Thanksgiving*** for the first time since July 30.

A couple of days before ***Thanksgiving Day,*** *Susan* went back to her job location in preparation for her return the first week of December. *Taavi* and *Susan* had a nice meal at an Irish pub, the first regular meal for *Susan* at a restaurant since July 31.

Also, the next day, they visited *Taavi's* mother *Loretta* at the nursing home where she was living.

This year ***Thanksgiving Day*** and ***Hanukkah*** (*Thanksgivukkah*) came during the same time of year—never to occur again for thousands of years! This year **Hanukkah** occurred November 27–December 5.

We had a great time of family food and fellowship during ***Thanksgiving!***

Hanukkah is celebrated by Jews and Messianic Believers in a sequence of eight days set aside to praise and thank God for His miraculous powers. It is also known in John 10:22-23 that Yeshua himself observed Chanukah.

John 10:22-23: 22"It was now winter, and **Jesus** was in **Jerusalem** at the time of **Hanukkah, the Festival of Dedication**. 23He was in the **Temple**, walking through the section known as *Solomon's Colonnade*." *[NLT]*

"The **Chanukah Story** (*Miracle in the Temple at Chanukah*) appears in the *Book of Maccabees*, which was written during the period between the First and Second Covenants (Old and New Testaments). The observance of the holiday is based upon the first war for religious freedom [around the years 169-172 BCE] when the Jewish people in Israel were ruled by Emperor Antiochus of Syria. He commanded everyone in his empire to worship idols. Antiochus even emptied **the Jewish Temple** in Jerusalem of all its holy treasures and set up an idol on the **altar of the Temple**. He further desecrated the **Temple** by bringing unclean animals into it. Soldiers of Antiochus then went to the small town of Mod'in and tried to force people there to worship idols, stop studying the **Torah**, give up observance of the **Sabbath**, and to stop following **the Commandments**. Those refusing to do so fled or were put to death."

"*Mattathias,* a member of a priestly family, along with his five sons and many others decided to band together and fight for their beliefs. *Mattathias* was old and soon died, but his son, *Judah Maccabee* (the "Hammer") became leader and his men were known as the **Maccabees**. They stood fast and defeated Antiochus' army, at that time the mightiest in the world."

The story continues in ***2 Maccabees 10:1-8***: 1"Maccabaeus and his companions, under the **Lord's guidance**, restored the **Temple** and the city, 2 and pulled down the altars erected by the foreigners in the market place, as well as the shrines. ₃They purified the **sanctuary** and built another **altar**; then, striking fire from flints and using this fire, the offered the **first sacrifice** for two years, **burning incense, lighting the lamps and setting out the loaves**...₅This day of the purification of the **Temple** on the very day on which the **Temple** had been profaned by the foreigners, the twenty-fifth of the same month, **Chislev**. ₆ They kept eight festal days with rejoicing, in the manner of the **feast of Shelters**...₇ Then carrying thyrsuses, leafy boughs and palms, they offered hymns to **him** who had brought the cleansing of **his own holy place** to a happy outcome. They also decreed by public edict, ratified by vote, that the whole Jewish nation should celebrate those same days every year." *[The New Jerusalem Bible]*

"There was an eternal lamp *(Ner Tamid)* in the **Temple** that had to be relit to make the **Temple** holy again, but there was only enough oil to burn for one day, and it would take eight days to prepare new olive oil. They lit **the eternal light** and a miracle happened—the lamp stayed lit for the eight days until the new oil had been prepared."

"Jews[and Messianic believers in **Yeshua**] today observe **Chanukah** by lighting one candle of the **Chanukiah** (a nine-branch menorah) each of the eight nights, by recounting the **Chanukah** story and sharing gifts. As Believers in **Messiah**, we can also take great joy in knowing that it is **Yeshua Who** is **the light of the world** for Jews and Gentiles alike, and through whom we have **the gift of salvation**." *(Miracle in the Temple at Chanukah)*

During this month, *Taavi* received inspiration for this song: "*Sing to God, Sing Praises to Adonai*" *[Psalm 68:32,33]*: 1. "My **Adonai**, my **Elohim**, my **Yeshua**; My **Messiah**, my **Heavenly King of Kings**, and **the Lord of Lords**. I will praise **You**, I will thank **You** forever and ev'rmore. **My Holy God, my Savior, Ruler of all my life**. " 2. "**The Most High God, the Creator, my Salvation. He is the Lord, the Counselor, Mighty and Holy Prince of Peace**. I will exalt **You**, I adore **You** for all Eternity. **Abba Father, the Holy One, Redeemer and my Friend**." *[© 2014 Malberg]*

Chapter 8

WINTER HOLIDAYS

Susan went back to work the first week in December, four to six weeks before she was originally scheduled to return. Again, the anointing of **the Holy Spirit** and the power of the prophetic ministry of the **_shofar_** helped rid the *Mohler's* home of the influence of outside sources of sin and evil and brought this miracle to bear upon them.

This was the first year for the *Mohlers* to light the **menorah.** *Rabbi Ya'akov*: "The *shammas* (a servant candle representing **Yeshua** as the light of the world) is used to light the other candles."

From *Rabbi Hector* : "Each evening during **_Hanukkah,_** family and friends gather to light the _hanukiyah_ with the appropriate number of candles. The branches of the _hanukiyah_ represent the eight days of **_Hannukkah_**, plus one *shamash* candle used to light the others.

...The appropriate number of candles are placed in the _hanukiyah_ from right to left, yet they are kindled by the _shamash_ from left to right.

On the first night of **_Hanukkah_**, after sundown, the _shamash_ (servant) candle is lit, which in turn is used to light the first candle in the **Menorah**. The second night, the _shamash_ is lit again and used to light the two right candles. This continues through the eight nights of the **_Hanukkah_**.

After the candles are lit, and the _shammas_ replaced, the following is said: '**We kindle these lights on account of the miracles, the deliverances and the wonders You performed for our fathers, by means of Your holy priests.** During all the eight days of **_Hanukkah_**, these lights are **Sacred,** and it is not permitted for us to make any use of them, but only to look at them, in order that we may give thanks unto **Your Name for Your miracles. Your deliverances, and Your wonders.**"

We read **_Psalm 30:1-12:_** 1"I will exalt you, **Lord** for you rescued me. You refused to let my enemies triumph over me...4 **Sing to the Lord**, all you godly ones**! Praise his holy name**. 5 ...Weeping may last through the night, but joy comes with morning... 7 **Your favor, o Lord**, made me as secure as a mountain. Then you turned away from me, and I was shattered. 8I cried out to you, **o Lord**. I begged the **Lord** for mercy, saying, 'What will you gain if I die, if sink into the grave?...Can my dust praise you? Can it tell of your faithfulness? 10 Hear me, **Lord**, and have mercy on me. **Help me o Lord**.' 11 **You** have turned my mourning into joyful dancing. **You** have taken away my clothes of mourning and clothed me with joy, 12 that I might sing praises to you and not be silent. **O Lord my God, I will give you thanks forever!**" [_NLT_]

Taavi and Susan enjoyed exchanging gifts each night of the lighting of the **Menorah.**

Later on in the month, around the time that traditional churches celebrate **Yeshua's birth, (**He was possibly conceived at this time), the Mohlers traded in their Dodge Van and purchased a Jeep, 4 WD, vehicle. They received full value for their van, which dealers' usually would discount because of an accident. This resulted in $1000. more for their down payment.

Total return of the first fruit offering of Yom Kippur was $11,000. Our **Yehovah** is faithful!!!

Later toward the end of the month, the Mohlers had fellowship with their children and grandchildren and enjoyed the family time.

To finish this chapter, there is some information about Christmas from "*Eliyah.com*":

"In ancient times, somewhere around 300 A.D., the Christians were trying to get more converts so they tried to make the **Messiah** more like idols found in sun worship—all under the guise of making **Him** more attractive to pagans.

Thus, they brought various elements of the December 25ᵗʰ 'feast of the unconquered sun' into their worship by saying that December 25ᵗʰ was actually the **Messiah's** birthday, which simply was not true.

This is the origin of Christmas and this is why we have various pagan-rooted traditions accompanying this observance."

Ephesians 5:11-14: 11 "Take no part in the futile works of darkness but, on the contrary, show them up for what they are. 12 The things which are done in secret are shameful even to speak of; 13 but anything shown up by **the light** will be illuminated 14 and anything illuminated is itself **a light.**" *(New Jerusalem Bible)*

Jeremiah 10: 1-5: 1 "Listen, **House of Israel**, to the word that **Yahweh** addresses to you. **Yahweh** says this' : " 2 'Do not learn the ways of the nations or take alarm at the heavenly signs, alarmed though the nations may be at them. 3 Yes, the customs of the peoples are quite futile: wood, nothing more, cut out of a forest, worked with a blade by a carver's hand, then embellished with silver and gold, then fastened with hammer and nails to keep it from moving. 5 Like scare-crows in a melon patch, they cannot walk. Have no fear of them: they can do no harm –nor any good either!' *[NLT]*

This is precisely why the *Mohlers* got rid of their ***Christmas*** trees and ornaments ($500 -$750).

They did purchase a yard inflatable: a 10 feet tall Dalmation dog with a **kippah** on his head and **the star of David** on its chest. They call him "*Sparky*". Everyone in the family, including our cockapoo dog, *Missy*, enjoyed the large dog display. *Rabbi Gomez* enjoyed it too (from the photograph I sent him)!!!

The **Lord Adonai** gave *Taavi* number seventy in a series of songs he has written since 2008: "*Yeshua God of Creation*" (*Genesis 1:1*): 1. "**Yeshua, the Lord of our Creation; Messiah, my Savior and Lord; Adonai**, both now and forever; **He** is the **King** of my life. 2. "**Yeshua, Dios de Creacion; Mesias, Salvador y Senor; Adonai**, ahora, siempre; **El es Rey** de mi vida. [accents optional] *[©2013 Malberg]*

Chapter 9

HISTORY OF RELATIONSHIP ENRICHMENT CENTER

Holly and *David* and daughter "*Rachel*" were privileged to be part of the celebration of the fourteenth anniversary of *R.E.C., Beit Tikkun* on January 11, 2014. There was a celebration of the Spanish Ministry *(Pastora Monica and Jorge)* and the R.E.C. congregations.

History of R.E.C., Beit Tikkun

Rabbi Hector and *Pastor Evelyn*, his wife began this congregation on January 11, 2000.

Rabbi Pastor Hector Gomez is a graduate of *Rhema Bible College, Simchat Torah Beit Midrash, and the International Center for Torah Studies.* He was an associate Pastor for two previous Centers for seven years each before starting the present ministry.

Our *Rabbi Hector Gomez* is a certified marriage counselor (*American Association of Christian Counselors*) and is certified with *Hillsborough County Marriage License Bureau.*

He and his wife, Evelyn, have been married for over 44 years and have helped cancel over 750 divorces!

The ministry of *Relationship Enrichment Center* is dedicated to restoring marriages and relationships, and to bring believers to the knowledge of their *Hebrew Roots* and their *Christian Faith.*

Biblical Truth is spoken at Beit Tikkun. There is **no** Talmud (rabbinic teachings) and **no** Christian doctrine.

The *Shema* is an important prayer to begin services on Thursday and **Shabbat** (Sabbath) on Saturday. *[Deut. 6:4]*

From a *Statement of Faith* by *Rabbi Hector* for R.E.C.: "The congregation believes that **Yeshua** is the **Son of God, the Messiah. He** is the **Word Who** became flesh and dwelt among us. *[John 1:1-14]*

We believe in the **Deity of Yeshua, his virgin birth.** *[Isaiah 9:6]*.

We believe that the **Bible** -- *Genesis through Revelation*—is the only inspired, infallible, and authoritative **Word of God.** *[2 Timothy 3:16]*

We believe that Man is a created being, made in the image of and likeness of **Elohim**, and that '... all have sinned and fall short of **the glory of God.'** *[Romans 3:23]*. **Salvation** is the **free gift of God** to man, apart from works and the **Torah. Salvation** is by grace through faith in **Yeshua**, producing works acceptable to **God.** *[Ephesians 2:8-9]*

We believe that the **Torah** (five books of Moses) is **God's teaching , instruction, and direction.** *[Exodus 19 & 20]*

We believe in **the baptism of the Holy Spirit** as the **gift of God** promised by **Yeshua** to all believers. [Matthew 3:11] We believe and embrace the **ministry of the Holy Spirit**...with **the gift of tongues** being one of **the manifestations of the Spirit.** *[Acts 19:1-7]*

We believe that believers are part of **Israel**, both natural and wild branches grafted into **Israel** by **the blood of the Messiah**. [Romans 11] We do believe that believers... have become part of, joint heirs of the promise, and members of the **Commonwealth of Israel.** *[Eph. 2:11]* *They have* the **Torah** written upon their hearts and minds according to the **New Covenant.** *[Romans 11: 11-24]*

We believe in ***the ingathering*** (**rapture**) of the entire congregation of **Israel**, once scattered to the nations. *[Hosea 9:17]*

Finally, We believe in the **Resurrection of the living and the dead**. Those who trust in **Yeshua** have received **Eternal Life in the Presence of God,** having their names written in the **Lamb's Book of Life** (*Heaven*). *[John 5:25-29]*

Those who do not believe experience **eternal separation from the Presence of God,** having **their names blotted out of the Lamb's book of Life** (*Hell*)." *[Rev. 20:12-15]*

Chapter 10

PURIM PLAY

Purim play

The middle of February, two spirit -filled Messianic Christian believers, *Roselie Rivera*, <u>*Director*</u> and *Jessica Pomales*, <u>*Dance Coordinator*</u>, began rehearsals for the Jewish Holiday of *Purim. David*, this book's author, was <u>*Narrator*</u>, *Mike Rivera*, <u>*Sound Coordinator*</u>, *Hylon Moon*, <u>*Light Coordinator*</u>, and *Rick*, <u>*Camera Coordinator*</u>. Of course, there were lots of supporting actors and actresses. There were many who helped create the stage , effects, and wardrobe designs.

Our *Purim* play was performed on March 15, 2014 at *R.E.C., Beit Tikkun*.

Here is a summary of the Jewish Holiday of **Purim**:

"It commemorates a time when the Jewish people living in **Persia** were saved from extermination. The story is told…in the *book of **Esther***. The heroes of the story are *Esther*, a beautiful young Jewish woman living in *Persia,* and her cousin, *Mordecai,* who raised her as if she were his daughter. *Esther* was taken to the house of *Ahasuerus* [reign: *BC 486-465],* **King of Persia**, to become part of his harem, and he loved her more than his other women and made her queen. But the *King* did not know that *Esther* was a **Jew**, because *Mordecai* told her not to reveal her nationality.

The villain of the story is *Haman,* an arrogant, egotistical advisor to the *King. Haman* hated *Mordecai* because *Mordecai* refused to bow down to *Haman,* so *Haman* plotted to destroy the **Jewish people**. His speech, in ***Esther 3:8,*** condemned the **Jews** to death.

Mordecai persuaded *Esther* to speak to the king on behalf of the **Jewish** people. This was dangerous… for *Esther*…because anyone who came into the **King's presence** without being summoned could be put to death, and she had not been summoned. *Esther* fasted for three days to prepare herself, then went into the *King*. He welcomed her. Later, she told him of **Haman's plot** against her people. The **Jewish** people were saved, and *Haman* was **hanged on the gallows** that had been prepared for *Mordecai.*" ***[Judaism 101]***

This time of *Purim* is a festive occasion to send out gifts of food and drink, and to make gifts to charity.

David and *Holly* were pleased that their children, "*David*" and "*Rachel*", and, their grandchildren, "*Tina*" and "*Sara*" attended **the Play.**

Chapter 11

DAVID'S SURGERY AND HEALING OF DISEASES

David's surgery

David developed **severe sinus symptoms** during the **rehearsals** of the *Purim* **play.** His prayer **request** to *Rabbi Hector* was to finish the **narration** of **the play** and to then have **surgery.**

He attempted to have *sinus surgery* on March 20, but had *chest pains,* and had to be admitted to the hospital. Fortunately, there were *no significant cardiac issues.*

So, he had to get another clearance from his *Cardiologist, Dr. Phillip,* and have another pre-op appointment by phone to have the **surgery** in April.

On April 6, *Rabbi Hector* spoke at another church about *Passover.* After the service, and after many people spoke to *Rabbi, David* asked for **prayer for his sinus surgery** the next day. *Rabbi* prayed for him in that *sanctuary.*

On April 6, evening, *David* made sure that his BP and pulse stayed at normal levels. So, he took medicine before midnight because his blood pressure was elevated. The following morning, David got up at 4:15 A.M. to take his antibiotic soap bath.

He and Susan left around 5 A.M. This time, David monitored his BP and pulse and took medicine, while Susan drove to the hospital. [The previous time, David made a mistake and drove himself, with Susan, to the hospital.]

Because *David* had to postpone his surgery previously, he was extremely anxious this time. Holly suggested that he and she say the *"spiritual warfare prayer"* that *Rabbi* had given us before. We both prayed before the nurse came into the room to prepare *David* for surgery.

One complicated thing that had to be resolved was *David's* **heart monitor**. Since there was a mix-up in scheduling, his device could not be turned off. The only way that the vibration could stop in his chest (prayerfully not in surgery) was to use **an auxiliary device**. After understanding how the unit worked, the nurse anesthetist, *John,* **put the auxiliary device in his pocket**. Fortunately, *the pre-heart attack warning device did not activate during surgery.*

Praise the Lord that *Dr. Mark* was able to complete **total sinus surgery ["_antrostomy_ and _maxillary_"]** and **he believed it to be successful!**

Healing of Diseases

After one of the **Sabbath** services, *David* asked *Rabbi* about **numbers**. *David* and *Holly* will **be married 39 years** this coming fall season. According to his chart, 39 = **disease**. But *Rabbi Hector* explained that " we want to trust **Yeshua** to grant **divine favor** and **complete healing** to *David* and *Holly*!!!"

James 3:13, 17-18: 3: 13 "If you are wise and understand **God's** ways, prove it by living an honorable life, doing good works with the humility that comes from wisdom." 3:17-18: 17 "But the wisdom from above is first of all pure. It is also peace loving, gentle at all times, and willing to yield to others. It is full of mercy and good deeds. It shows no favoritism and is always sincere. 18 And those who are peacemakers will plant seeds of peace and reap a harvest of righteousness." *[NLT]*

Psalm 103: 1-5: 1 "Let all that I am praise the **Lord**; with my whole heart, I will praise **his holy name**. 2 "Let all that I am praise the **Lord**; may I never forget the good things he does for me. 3 "**He** forgives all my sins and heals all of my diseases. 4 "**He** redeems me from death and crowns me with love and tender mercies. 5 "**He** fills my life with good things. My youth is renewed like the eagle's." *[NLT]*

Chapter 12

PASSOVER AND THE LORD'S SUPPER

Passover

David and Holly attended their first *Shabbat Hagadol* (Great Sabbath) with the *Parsha* (Torah portion) "Acharei Mot" (*After the Death)* on April 12. Also, the *Malbergs* gave their *First Fruit Offering* at this time.

Leviticus 16:1-2: 1 "The **Lord** spoke to Moses after the death of Aaron's two sons, who died after they entered the **Lord's presence** and burned the wrong kind of fire before him. 2 The **Lord** said to Moses, 'Warn your brother Aaron, not to enter the **Most Holy Place** behind the inner curtain whenever he chooses; if he does, he will die. For the **Ark's cover—the place of atonement—**is there, **and I myself am present in the cloud** above the **atonement cover.**" *[NLT]*

Rabbi Gomez also shared some information relating to the **blood moons** and *these heavenly events* **significance** to the **state of Israel** in the future.

Psalm 102: 15-16: 15 "Then the nations will tremble before **the Lord.** The kings of the earth will tremble before his glory. 16 For **the Lord** will rebuild Jerusalem. **He will appear in his glory.**" *[NLT]*

The next day the *Malbergs and daughter* attended *David and Holly's* first *Passover Seder* at "Hebrew Roots Bible College" with *Rabbi Ralph.*

The first Passover: *Exodus 12: 21-25:* 21 'Then Moses called all the elders of Israel together and said to them,' "Go pick out a lamb or young goat for each of your families, and slaughter the **Passover** animal. 22 Drain the blood into a basin. Then take a bundle of hyssop branches and dip it into the blood. Brush the hyssop across the top and sides of the doorframes of your houses. And no one may go out through the door until morning. 23 For the **Lord** will pass through the land to strike down the Egyptians. But when he sees the blood on the top and sides of the doorframe, the Lord will pass over your home. He will not permit his death angel to enter your house or strike you down... 25 When you enter the land the Lord has promised to give you, you will continue to observe this ceremony."

Israel's Exodus from Egypt: *Exodus 12:31-34:* [31] 'Pharaoh sent for Moses and Aaron during the night.' "Get out!" he ordered. "Leave my people—and take the rest of the Israelites with you! Go and worship the Lord as you have requested…[34] The Israelites took their bread dough before yeast was added. They wrapped their kneading boards in their cloaks and carried them on their shoulders."

The Seder meal: **"The Haggadah"** is a book that guides the family through the course of the meal. **The Seder plate** has *1. Roasted Shank bone of Lamb*. 2. *Hard boiled egg*. 3. *Bitter Herbs* cut into small pieces, or fresh grated horseradish. 4. *Charoses*: a mixture of finely cut apples, nuts and cinnamon mixed with a little wine. 5. *Karpas:* either parsley, celery or potatoes may be used. 6. *Chazeres*: romaine lettuce or fresh horseradish.

Other items: *Three Matzohs* wrapped separately. *Wine*—decanter with wine goblet for each setting. *Salt water*—used by all. *Cup of Elijah*—a large goblet filled with wine near the center of the table. *Pillow* – placed on another chair close to the left arm of the leader. [*Coffees of Maxwell House: Passover Haggadah*]

The most important items are the *roasted shank bone of lamb*, the *karpas* and the *Matzohs*.

The Lord's Supper

On the *Passover Sabbath*, April 19, 5774 (2014), *Rabbi Gomez* chose twelve men from the congregation to participate at the **Lord's table**. *David* was delighted to represent one of the disciples.

**Luke 22:7-21**: 7 'Now the **Festival of Unleavened Bread** arrived when the **Passover lamb** is sacrificed. 8 **Jesus** sent <u>Peter</u> and <u>John</u> ahead and said', "Go and prepare the **Passover meal**, so we can eat together." [**Yeshua** gave them specific instructions on who they were to contact and where was the _guest room_ upstairs.]

...15 '**Jesus** said', "**I have been eager to eat this** <u>Passover meal</u> with you before my **suffering** begins. 16 For I tell you now that **I won't eat this meal again until its meaning is fulfilled in the Kingdom of God.**" 17 'Then **he took took a cup of wine and gave thanks to God** for it. Then he said', 'Take this and share it among yourselves. 18 For **I will not drink wine again until the Kingdom of God** has come.' 19 '**He took some bread and gave thanks** to **God** for it. The **he broke it in pieces and gave it to the disciples saying**', "This **is my body, which is given to you. Do this to remember me.**"

20 '**After supper he took another cup of wine and said**', "**This cup is the new covenant** between **God** and his people—an agreement confirmed with **my blood** , which is poured out as **a sacrifice** for you." _[NLT]_

This is why we have **<u>communion a</u>**t our **<u>Sabbath feast</u>** each week after **<u>sundown Friday</u>**.

**Leviticus 23: 3:** 3 "You have six days each week for your ordinary work, but **the seventh day** is **a Sabbath day** of <u>complete rest</u>, an official day for <u>holy assembly</u>. It is **the Lord's Sabbath day**, and it must be observed wherever you live." _[NLT]_

EPILOGUE

Betrothal

Our congregation of *R.E.C., Beit Tikkun*, rejoiced in the betrothal of *Sarah Gomez* and Alex *McCarthy*. *Alex* asked *Rabbi Gomez* for permission to begin dating *Sarah*, which culminated in the betrothal ceremony and a future marriage ceremony in 2015.

Pastor Nick of *Beit Tahila* performed the ceremony on **Shabbat, Shavuot,** and *Pastor Evelyn Gomez'* birthday on June 7, 2014.

Here the parts of "The Betrothal" *(Messianic Teacher, Glen Kay ©2010)*

1) The ***"Shiddukhin"*** is the first step of the marriage process. This is the selecting of the bride. In ancient Israel, the father of the groom selected a bride for his son. In the United States, a young man, *Alex*, asked *Rabbi Gomez* for his daughter's, *Sarah*, hand in marriage. ***Genesis 24:2-4:*** 2"…Place your hand under my thigh: 3 I am going to make you swear to **Yahweh, God of heaven**, and **God of the earth,** that you will…4 …go to my native land and my own kinsfolk to choose a wife for my son Isaac." ***[New Jerusalem Bible]***

2) ***"Ketubah"*** includes the the conditions and provisions of the proposed marriage:

   The groom promises to support his future wife and the bride stipulates the contents of her dowry (financial status).

3) The ***"Mohar" (Bridal payment)***

   It is the gift paid by the groom to the bride's family (but, in the end, belongs to the bride). Her status was changed and she is set free from her parent's household.

   In ***Genesis 24: 52-53:*** 52"…*Abraham's servant* bowed to the ground before **Yahweh.** 53 He brought out silver and gold ornaments and clothes which he gave to *Rebekah;* he also gave rich presents to her brother [*Laban*] and to her mother [*Bethuel*]. ***[New Jerusalem Bible]***

4) ***"Mikveh" (Ritual immersion)***

   It was common for the bride and groom (separately) to take a ritual immersion. This would have been done prior to entering the formal betrothal period, and was a symbol of spiritual cleansing.

5) ***"Illustration in Messiah's Bride"***

   We were selected by the Father to be His Beloved Son's loving precious bride:

   Ephesians !:4: 4 "Even before **he** made the world, **God** loved us and chose us in **Christ** to be holy and without fault in **his eyes.**"[NLT]

6) ***"Erusin" (Betrothal)***

   The purpose of this period is to prepare the bride and groom to enter into the covenant of marriage. In the Jewish culture, a "get" is necessary to annul the contract.

They both appear under the *Huppah* (canopy) and in public where they express their intention of being betrothed (engaged). While under the *Huppah,* items of value are exchanged—rings, and a cup of wine was shared to seal the betrothal agreement. In the case of *Sarah and Alex,* parents of both had some prayers for their children.

The period of betrothal lasts (usually) for one year. During this time, the couple is considered married, but they do not have sexual relations; and, live separately until the end of the betrothal. Also, the groom will prepare a home for his bride. And the bride will prepare her wedding garments.

We see this beautifully illustrated in the lives of *Yoseph and Miriam,* our **Lord's** parents: ***Matt. 1: 18 – 25:*** 18 "This is how **Jesus the Messiah** was born. His mother, Mary, was engaged to be married to Joseph. But before the marriage took place, while she was still a virgin, she became pregnant through the power of the **Holy Spirit.** 19 Joseph, her fiancé, was a good man and did not want to disgrace her publicly, so he decided to break the engagement quietly. 20 As he considered this, an **angel of the Lord** appeared to him in a dream." 'Joseph, son of David,' the angel said, 'do not be afraid to take Mary as your wife. For the child within her was conceived by the **Holy Spirit.** 21 And she will have a son, and you are to name him **Jesus**, for he will save his people from their sins.' 24 "When Joseph woke up, he did as the **angel of the Lord** commanded and took Mary as his wife. 25 But he did not have sexual relations with her until her son was born. And Joseph named him **Jesus**." *[NLT]*

3500 years ago, fifty days after the first Passover in Egypt, Moses went up to Mt. Sinai and received the *Torah,* God's first teaching and instruction to the children of Israel. These were blueprints for Israel and all mankind on how to live and conduct their lives.

2000 years ago, on the Jewish holiday of *Shavuot,* exactly fifty days after Passover, the disciples," together in one accord and one place", received the Holy Spirit. *[Acts 2:2]*

Unfortunately, today, many Jewish people do not read the scriptures regularly or rely on their rabbis to interpret Scripture for them. Because of this, "the important Messianic prophecies are either omitted or denied."*[Messianic Bible]*

"At *the Festival of Harvest [Weeks]*, when you present the first of your new grain [offering] to the Lord, you must call an official day for holy assembly, and you may do no ordinary work on that day." *[Numbers 28:26]* *[NLT]*

"The celebration of the **Torah** and the **Ruach** [**Ruach Hakodesh**], ...[and] the offering of thanksgiving to **God** for the first fruits...**God** wants us to know **His** ways and be empowered by his **Ruach** [**Spirit**] to live holy lives, bearing much fruit in **Him**." *[Rabbi Hector Gomez]*

Ezekiel 36: 26-27: 26"And **I** will give you a new heart, and I will put a new spirit in you. **I** will take out your stony, stubborn heart and give you a tender, responsive heart. 27 And **I** will put my **Spirit** in you so that you will follow **my decrees** and be careful to obey **my regulations**." *[NLT]*

On the Sunday following **Shavuot**, the *Malbergs* attended a graduation ceremony at Clermont, Florida, along with "*Rachel*" and *Diane, Holly's* friend, who was visiting. They had completed an "*Ancient Foundations*" class with *Hebrew Bible College. Rabbi Ralph* spoke about the "*Prodigal Son*" and the connection to the **Church.**

Also, David and Holly had given the first of their "*first fruit offering*" the day before, June 7, which resulted in multiple blessings the following week.

David's mother *Loretta (Nemire)* passed away on May 23 this year. A few minutes after her passing, there was a fantastic meteor display in the heavens.

Here is a song that *David* wrote a few weeks before his mother's passing:

The King of the Universe

D.E.M. Rev. 11:15 David Malberg

moderato

Piano

Seek the Lord with all your heart and your mind. He gives you peace and joy for you to find.

He re-freshes with a song a-long the way, as we wor-ship Him each and ev'-ry day.

We are as-sailed from each and ev'-ry side, but we look to Ye-shu-a as our guide.

The Lord puts whole Truth into our hands to share with oth-ers who are liv-ing in the Land.

"The King of the Universe": "Seek the **Lord** with all your heart and your mind. **He** gives peace and joy for you to find. **He** refreshes with a song along the way as we worship **Him** each and every day." "We are assailed from each and every side, but we look to **Yeshua** as our guide. The **Lord** puts whole **Truth** into our hands to share with others who are living in the land." Chorus: " **Our King is Holy. Lift His Name on High. He** will satisfy. **He is Creator**." [title: *Rev. 11:15*] *[©2014 Malberg]*

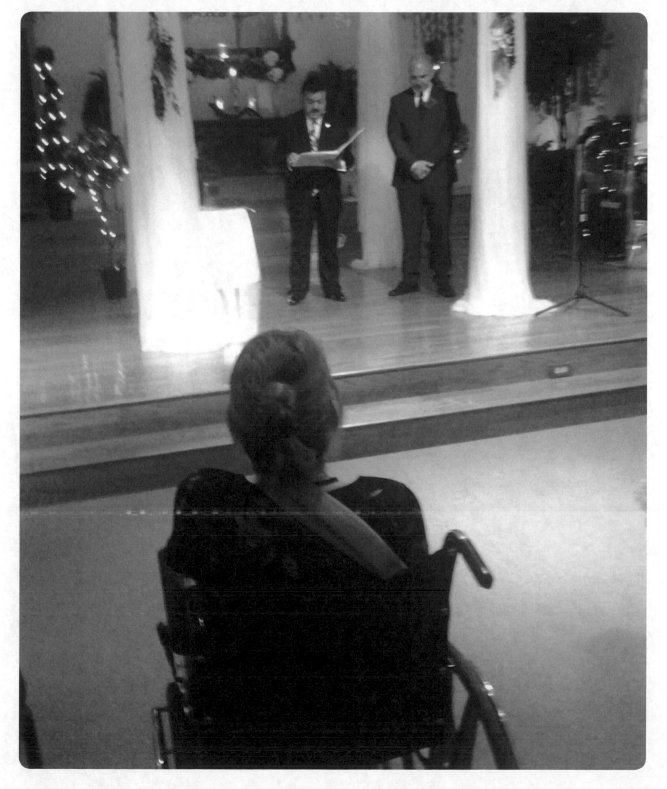

A **wedding** took place at *Relationship Enrichment Center, Beit Tikkun* on June 22. *Eric,* <u>Rabbi</u> and <u>Evelyn's</u> eldest son, and his fiancée, *Katrina* exchanged vows of **Holy Matrimony**. *Rabbi Gomez* performed the ceremony. It was a blessed **Messianic** event. A beautiful reception took place afterward at an outstanding local restaurant.

The Shema [Deut. 6:4] is said or sung at the end of the **Sabbath feast,** at the beginning of **Torah Studies** and during **Shabbat.** This *Hebrew Pledge of Allegiance* represents a particular limb of your body. Every time a word of the **Shema** is spoken a particular limb is strengthened. [*Path of the Just, Rabbi M.C. Luzzato,* 18th century Italy.]

"Sh'ma Yisrael, Adonai Eloheinu, Adonai Echad. Baruch shem, K'vod malchuto, l'olam vaed."

"Hear O **Israel, The Lord our God. The Lord is One. Blessed be His Name. His Kingdom is forever,** and forever more." **(Mark 12:29)**

I would like to close this book with the **Priestly blessing (<u>Aaronic prayer</u>)** that the father *(David)* prays after the **Sabbath feast** and our *Rabbi Hector* prays after *"Torah Studies"* and *"Shabbat":*

"Yevarech'cha **Adonai** v'yishmerech Ya'er **Adonai** panav elecha biyechuneka **Yissah Adonai** panav eleycha veyasem lecha **shalom.**"

"May **the Lord** <u>bless you and protect you.</u> May **the Lord** <u>smile on you and be gracious to you.</u> May **the Lord** <u>show you</u> **his favor** <u>and give you</u> **his peace.**" *[<u>Numbers 6:24-26</u>] [<u>NLT</u>]*

Shalom b'Yeshua [Peace in Messiah (Jesus)]

Rabbi/Pastor Hector and Evelyn Gomez and David C. Malberg

Printed in the United States
by Baker & Taylor Publisher Services